THE
AWKWARD
SEASON

THE

AWKWARD SEASON

PRAYERS FOR LENT

PAMELA C. HAWKINS

UPPER
ROOM BOOKS®
NASHVILLE

THE AWKWARD SEASON: Prayers for Lent
Copyright © 2009 by Pamela C. Hawkins
All rights reserved.

The Upper Room Web site: www.upperroom.org

UPPER ROOM®, UPPER ROOM BOOKS®, and design logos are trademarks owned by The Upper Room®, a ministry of GBOD®, Nashville, Tennessee. All rights reserved.

Scripture quotations are from the New Revised Standard Version Bible, copyright 1989, Division of Christian Education of the National Council of the Churches of Christ in the United States of America. Used by permission. All rights reserved.

Most scripture selections are from The Revised Common Lectionary. Copyright © 1992 The Consultation on Common Texts (CCT) admin. Augsburg Fortress Publishers. Used by permission.

Cover design: Left Coast Design, Portland, OR / www.lcoast.com
Cover image: Jill Battaglia, Istockphotos.com
Interior design: Buckinghorse Design / www.buckinghorsedesign.com
Illustrations: Jim Osborn
First printing: 2009

Library of Congress Cataloging-in-Publication Data

Hawkins, Pamela C.
   The awkward season : prayers for Lent / Pamela C. Hawkins.
      p. cm.
   ISBN 978-0-8358-9997-0
1. Lent—Prayers and devotions   I. Title.
   BV85.H43 2009
   242'.34—dc22

                               2008055885

Printed in the United States of America

for my father,
Leon W. Cunningham

contents

acknowledgments

Almost fifteen years ago my path crossed that of Rueben P. Job. Since that grace-filled intersection, Bishop Job has taught me to pray in more ways than I had ever imagined possible. I thank him for guiding me into prayer, time and again, no matter the season. On many a day as I wrote this little book, Rueben's calming prayers came to mind. And so, I give God thanks for Rueben's life of prayer and for his prayers for me.

I am also deeply grateful to my husband, Ray, and son, Erick, who have weathered the creative storms that come and go during my writing seasons. Often, when words for a prayer seem stuck, either Erick or Ray will loosen them with an encouraging word or a sweet touch. Love is often like this.

A word of gratitude is due, as well, to my colleagues at The Upper Room. Thanks to Lynne Deming for vocational encouragement; to John Mogabgab for generous guidance; to Robin Pippin and Kathleen Stephens for creative and patient counsel; and to Beth Richardson, Jerry Haas, and Susan Ruach for wise and caring friendship.

And to my extended church family in Nashville, Tennessee, I send words of thanks. To Sandra Griggs and the community she pastors at Glendale United

Methodist Church for providing quiet space throughout this project. To my Tuesday morning covenant friends Libby Baxter, Donna Williard, Lisa Gwock, Margaret Tocknell, Susan Groseclose, and Martha Lott, with whom I have shared life's seasons for over twenty years. And to my pastor and lifelong friend, Peter van Eys, of Calvary United Methodist Church, whose love for God's world and God's people never falters.

Finally, I give God particular thanks for my father, Leon Cunningham. In the past year I have watched him navigate the most awkward season of all—the long "first year" since my mother's death. More than he can ever know, he has taught me the best lessons of all: those about grace, forgiveness, love, and generosity. I dedicate this work to him.

introduction

For as long as I can remember, Lent has seemed an awkward season. Although I have never been confused about where Lent leads—to Easter—I have often been unsure about how best to follow its path.

Lent is a holy season of the church that begins in the middle of the week, on a Wednesday instead of a Sunday. For my whole church life Sunday has been the starting place for most important seasons. Sundays are on my worship radar. But Ash Wednesday often sneaks up on me in my busy life, and I am behind on the Lenten journey before I even know it.

If the date of Easter were not a moving target, Lent might not seem so awkward to navigate. But unlike Christmas, which, like north on a compass, always points to one resting place, December 25, Easter moves around. And because Lent is attached to Easter by forty days, its date also moves around. It's an awkward, seemingly unpredictable point to track.

Now, one could imagine that these familiar forty days of Lent might serve as signposts for Christian pilgrims like me. In my tradition, forty is a number with weight and meaning. Moses and the Hebrew people spent forty years in the desert; Jesus spent forty days in the wilderness; the church spends forty days in Lent. So I used to think that all I needed to do was count backward from Easter to "day forty," and I would find my feet firmly planted at the Lenten starting line. Awkwardly, that is not so.

When we count backward from Easter Sunday, the fortieth day is not Ash Wednesday. Why not? Because the forty days of Lent do not even include Sundays. This is, for me, one of the most awkward contours of Lent—Lent does not include the one day of the week on which, historically, most Christian communities gather for worship. Sundays "do not count" in the forty days of Lent in my tradition. Sundays are *in* Lent but not *of* it.

The early church fathers and mothers designated Sundays as days for celebrating the Resurrection. Therefore, Sundays are feast days in the church, and the spiritual practice of fasting is not part of Sunday's rhythm. But Lent is the season leading up to the Resurrection, and fasting is a central spiritual discipline associated with the season. Lenten days are fast days in the church. Yet even with these historical road maps, the contemporary journey through Lent still can be awkward.

Lent has curves and contours, rites and rituals that can confuse those who try to follow its path toward Easter morning. Some Christians begin the Lenten journey with a cross-shaped smudge of ash on their foreheads—that is, if they can remember to mark Ash Wednesday on their calendars. Some choose to give up a habit or pleasure as a gesture of *penitence*—a word many contemporary Christians consider foreign.

Some of us simply travel the season of Lent by carefully stepping over it from one Sunday to the next, gathering up curious pieces of scripture along the way, and making a final festive leap straight from Palm Sunday to Easter Sunday, bypassing Holy Week's difficult and tragic turns. Others of us move more slowly, guided by daily prayers or daily mass, missing not one single Holy Week way station toward the Cross—not Maundy Thursday, Good Friday, or Holy Saturday, as brutal as they are for all who dare to love Jesus.

The good news for us, unconfused and clear, is that no particular Lenten journey is more perfect or right than another. Our journey to Easter is ours and no one else's. No other person can travel there for us, nor can we for them; and yet we all will end up at the same destination—Easter morning outside the walls of Jerusalem! And because we have adjusted our lives a little or a lot to follow Jesus through the ups and downs, the deserts and roads of Lent, we can also count on one other truth that will become clear when the dust settles: we all will find ourselves at a different place than where we began.

The purpose of this little prayer book is to offer Christian pilgrims a path to follow through Lent—a prayer path, to be exact. The pattern of prayer in these pages is intended to be clear and straightforward, not awkward or confusing. For each day you choose to use this book, you will find one way in (prayer), one center (scripture), and one way out (prayer). You cannot make a wrong turn in this book, and no detour or delay will keep you from arriving at Easter. Still, I hope that you will make plans for the full journey, spending as much time as you can spare with the One who longs to be your companion in this season and always.

May the God of traveling mercy

become your guide in Lent and beyond.

Amen.

HOW TO USE THIS BOOK

For any day during Lent, from Ash Wednesday through Holy Saturday, you will find one pattern of daily prayer (a daily office) in this book. Turn to the day of the week on which you wish to pray, and start there. The prayers are shaped around daily themes prompted by the psalm for the day. The scripture readings, one for each day, are taken from the ecumenical lectionary for the season of Lent with one exception: the reading for Holy Saturday.

For some readers, the experience of repeating the same daily prayers may seem, at first, dull and uninventive. Our culture bombards us with constant change, setting an expectation that we can navigate quickly and nimbly through new images, proficiencies, and ideas. To set an expectation that we will, instead, return week after week to the same words, prayers, and patterns may feel more like work of the mind rather than gift of the Spirit. If this is how we approach these prayers for Lent—as work—then, perhaps surprisingly, we begin in exactly the right place and attitude to use a daily office of prayer. This little book *is* about sharing in some work, for the word *office* finds its root in the Latin word *opus*, meaning "work." By joining in the rhythm of shared daily prayer found in *The Awkward Season*, we share in *opus dei,* or "the work of God."

In what better way can we be companions through the awkwardness of Lent than to know that on any given day, we will all begin at the same place of prayer? Every Sunday, no matter what distractions or detours have led us elsewhere the day or week before, any who return to prayer on a Sunday in Lent will return to the same place and join the journey again. The same will be true on any Monday or any Tuesday. Like a trail or path worn clear and deep by travelers heading toward the same destination, our path with God deepens and changes as we share our journey of faith through prayer, reading of scripture, and companionship with God and neighbor. What might have, at first, appeared shallow or dull in sameness may instead be experienced as deepened and illumined through constancy. This is an offering of daily prayer.

ORDER OF DAILY PRAYER

In this book the order of daily prayer includes the following:

Invocation: The invocation is an opening prayer that guides us to call upon the Lord and to enter expectantly into God's life-giving and forgiving presence. Words from the Psalms are used for these opening prayers.

Prayer of Confession: A prayer of confession, rooted in the day's theme and psalm, is offered. Confessing to God where we have fallen short of the mark of Christian living leads us inward. Through confession we ask for God's help to clear out obstacles of heart, mind, and deed that clutter our ability to be fully present to God and God's life-altering ways. In confession we spend introspective time examining—always in the light of God's merciful and forgiving grace—where we have done harm to others, to ourselves, and to creation. Confession permits us prayer space in which to acknowledge our human limitations, and then to enter holy space in which our hearts can be gently cleansed and newly created.

Lent is a season of the church year in which confession holds a prominent place in personal and corporate prayer. Scattered over the entire Lenten landscape are stories from scripture about sin and death, temptation and trial, doubt and disbelief, betrayal and denial. These accounts of the darker side of our human condition illumine our need to place ourselves in God's healing, redeeming light. We know about this light. It is the light of Easter morning toward which we journey. But first we must walk with Jesus through the dark ditches, dry deserts, and half-truths that impede our movement. Prayers of confession can help clear a way for us.

Scripture Reading: One scripture reading is given for each day of Lent. This means, for example, that on the first Thursday of the season (the day after Ash Wednesday), you will read only the one passage from scripture listed for the First Thursday of Lent. Then, on the following Thursday, you will read only the passage for the Second Thursday, and so on for each day of the season. The passages come from the readings for Lent in the ecumenical lectionary. They support the overarching themes of the season of Lent, not necessarily the individual themes of the days. Scriptures for Sundays come from the Revised Common Lectionary so that any readers who wish to do so may read along with the Sunday lectionary. A Guide to Daily Scripture Readings, including the Sunday lectionary readings, is given on page 25.

The scripture readings are recommended, not required, readings. If a different passage comes to mind or you find a selection from another Lenten resource or practice, feel free to use that passage instead. This book is designed to support rather than dictate your Lenten journey. Whatever scripture you are led to use, read it slowly and meditatively. Read with an open heart, expecting that God has something for you to receive as you take time to center on the Word. If possible, read the passage more than once.

When you have completed your reading, spend some time in silent reflection about what this reading prompts in you. What emotions, memories, questions, or insights arise? You will find a reminder in the day's prayers to observe a time of silent reflection. Resist the temptation to bypass or rush through this silence. Often it is in silence that God's presence becomes most clear.

Prayers of Intercession: Praying for others, intercessory prayer, is the next movement in this daily office. Prayers of intercession turn our gaze outward, beyond our own needs, and return us to the world that God profoundly loves. Intercessory prayers begin with God, upon whom our prayer life must be centered; otherwise the depth of need and brokenness in the world would overwhelm our praying hearts. But when we center our lives in God and pray as Jesus taught, there is no need too great or circumstance too raw for which we are not equipped to pray.

A prayer of intercession is given for each day, followed by a set of suggested intercessory categories. You may, of course, add to or replace any of these prayer emphases with others of your own.

Closing Prayer of Thanksgiving: Words of gratitude are offered in brief closing prayers. We acknowledge and give thanks to the ever-present, always-renewing Holy Spirit who has been, is, and will be with us on our journey of faith.

Blessing: As a blessing before we go, another line from the day's psalm is given.

praying with a finger labyrinth (optional)

Open the flap at the back of this book, and you'll see a finger labyrinth. The labyrinth is provided as an optional prayer tool for those who wish to try it. You do not have to use it with this prayer book. You may follow the daily prayers with or without it.

The finger labyrinth is offered for two reasons:

1. Some people find that a prayer tool such as a labyrinth strengthens and deepens their practice of prayer.

2. I believe there is a lovely synchronized pattern between the prayer movement through Lent—Confession (inward journey), Reflection on scripture (centering), and Intercession (outward journey)—and the prayer movement through a labyrinth—Releasing (inward journey), Receiving (centering), and Returning (outward journey).

To learn more about the labyrinth and how it can support your prayers during Lent, read pages 21–24 and 111–12.

The Labyrinth and Prayer

A labyrinth is simply a design for a path. Often confused with mazes, which are intended to trick those who try to figure them out, labyrinths are designed to be clearly followed from beginning to end.

Every labyrinth pattern, whether created for walking by foot or tracing by finger, has only one way in, one center, and one way out. There is nothing in a labyrinth path to confuse, trick, or lose the one who follows it.

Labyrinths have been used for centuries as paths for meditation and prayer in many different faith traditions. As with any other prayer path or tool, a labyrinth simply offers an opening through which we seek, meet, and spend time with God.

Lent, pilgrimage, and the Labyrinth

During Lent, the New Testament scriptures place Christians with Jesus on a path to Jerusalem. The journey that stretches before us will not be an easy one. It will be a pilgrim's journey. The path will wind through temptation, struggle, sacrifice, and love. Self-examination, confession, conflict, self-discovery, betrayal, and compassion will pave the way. Eyes will be opened, lives will be set free, and hearts will be jump-started. Some fellow pilgrims will slip and lose their footing, choosing to stay where they fall. Others will slip and fall, choosing to stay on their knees before getting up and moving forward.

Christian pilgrimage has always been risky. As far back as the tenth century, faithful Christians were expected to travel at least once in a lifetime to their spiritual home, Jerusalem. But before long, war and politics made Holy Land pilgrimage too dangerous and costly for most Christians, so early church leaders designed cathedral labyrinths—stone or marble patterns built into the floors—on which Christian pilgrims could make a symbolic journey to Jerusalem by walking the narrow design.

Of course, not everyone could travel to a cathedral labyrinth, so over the years, people from many different religious traditions began to design local and personal labyrinths out of bricks, grass, flowers, paper, wood, canvas, and even on computer screens. Today, prayer labyrinths of all sizes and materials can be found around the world. Some are large enough to span a church nave or a city parking lot, while others are small enough to fit inside a pocket or a book.

As with all prayer practices and tools, the labyrinth offers a prayer path for any time or season of life. Yet, for me, there is a remarkable and useful alignment between prayers for Lent and prayers for a labyrinth. Both Lent and the labyrinth are about faith journeys. Both have clear beginnings, centers, and clear endings. But there is more.

Traditionally, when praying the labyrinth, Christians follow three classic stages or movements. First, as we enter the labyrinth path, we are invited to *release*, to let go of all that stands in our way and distracts us from God—our destination and center. As we move toward the center of the labyrinth, we are invited to be mindful of obstacles that may prevent us from being open to God's presence and leading. Second, as we reach the center of the labyrinth, we are invited to *receive* what God desires for us. It may be a word or a nudge, a comfort or call. At the center, we rest and reflect upon what God chooses to reveal to us. Third, as we go out from the center on the same path by which we entered, we are invited to *return* to the world, open to new ways of living, being, and praying.

Similarly, when praying through Lent, Christians often follow three classic spiritual practices. First, as we enter the season we are called upon to confess, to *release* our hold on all that clutters, strains, and stains our relationship with God, neighbor, and self. Next, in order to find our spiritual center again, we pray to *receive* a word for our lives from the Word of Life. And so we stake the season's prayers into the centering ground of scripture. Finally, as we prepare our lives to *return* to the world as disciples of the risen Christ, we must look up and out in prayer at the whole hurting creation that has been entrusted to us by the One who taught us to pray and to love.

If you decide that you would like to use a labyrinth to support your Lenten prayers this year, a finger labyrinth is provided on the inside of the flap at the back of this book. See page 111 for instructions.

A Guide to Daily Scripture Readings

All the scripture readings in these daily prayers have been taken from readings for Lent in the Revised Common Lectionary. A lectionary is a suggested order for reading scripture through the Christian seasons and year. The Revised Common Lectionary is a three-year cycle of readings (Year A, Year B, Year C) and is just one of several available sources and traditions offering guidance for scripture selection in prayer and worship.

In *The Awkward Season*, the readings for weekdays intersperse scriptures from all three years (A, B, and C) of this ecumenical lectionary. The readings for the Sundays in Lent include the Gospel reading for each lectionary year on the assigned day, so that this little prayer book might serve as a companion resource in churches as well as a personal resource for individuals.

To identify the Sunday readings for Year A, Year B, and Year C, follow this guide:

If Lent is in the year:	Read the Sunday passage for:
2011, 2014, 2017, 2020, etc.	Year A
2012, 2015, 2018, 2021, etc.	Year B
2010, 2013, 2016, 2019, etc.	Year C

DAILY LENTEN PRAYERS

The following daily prayers for Lent invite us to return, week after week, to a repeated pattern and practice of prayer. For any day of the week (except Ash Wednesday, Maundy Thursday, Good Friday, and Holy Saturday) the prayers of invocation, confession, intercession, thanksgiving, and blessing remain the same. Only the scripture reading changes. Returning to the same words of prayer anchors us in the otherwise awkward swells and currents of a culture that distracts and pushes us away from our relationship with God.

Repetition returns us to something constant; repetition in prayer returns us to communion with God, who is constant. Repeated daily prayer that is *shared* can help us resist becoming disconnected not only from the One to whom we pray but also from the ones with and for whom we pray.

No matter who we are or where we've been the day or week before, we all begin again at the same place, connecting with our neighbors—known and unknown—those who pray the same words as we do and those for whom we pray.

ASH WEDNESDAY

CLEARING

INVOCATION

Create in me a clean heart,
O God,
and put a new and right
spirit within me.

—Psalm 51:10

PRAYER OF CONFESSION

O God, who makes all things new,
new stars, new dust, new life;
take my heart,
every hardened edge and measured beat,
and create something new in me.
I need your newness, God,
the rough parts of me made smooth;
the stagnant, stirred;
the stuck, freed;
the unkind, forgiven.
And then, by the power of your Spirit,
I need to be turned toward Love again.
Amen.

SCRIPTURE READING

Read the passage for the day silently or out loud. Read slowly; do not hurry. If you have time, read it again. Then spend some time in silent reflection about any questions or insights the reading prompted. What catches your attention? What word or phrase stops you? What images stay with you? What might God wish for you to receive from this reading?

Ash Wednesday—Matthew 6:1-6, 16-21

SILENT REFLECTION

PRAYERS OF INTERCESSION

O Christ, our Alpha and Omega;
O Christ, our beginning and our end.
Help me to see where something new is needed,
longed for,
breaking through.
Help me become an instrument,
a lever,
a voice for
what is hoped for but has not yet come to be.
Amen.

PRAY

- For renewed commitment to stewardship of creation
- For new discoveries in research
- For new beginnings
- For what is on your heart this day

CLOSING PRAYER OF THANKSGIVING

O Holy Spirit, I thank you
for the life-giving light you bring to my days
and the life-saving grace you bring to my life.
Grant to me new eyes to see,
new ears to listen,
a new heart ready to hold the love that is Christ's love.
Amen.

BLESSING

Have mercy on me, O God,
     according to your steadfast love.

          —Psalm 51:1a

THURSDAYS
OF LENT

LONGING

Return to these pages each Thursday (except Maundy Thursday) and begin to pray.

INVOCATION

As a deer longs for flowing streams,
      so my soul longs for you, O God.
My soul thirsts for God,
      for the living God.
When shall I come and behold
      the face of God?

                  —Psalm 42:1-2

PRAYER OF CONFESSION

Sometimes, O God, my thirst for you
is pushed aside, ignored,
or simply quenched by something other—
something more reasonable,
something more popular—than you.
But you never go away,
never stop,
never leave the depths of me.
Like an underground spring,
you are fresh and free,
breaking through.
Help me prepare a place for you in the caverns of my soul.
Amen.

SCRIPTURE READING

Read the passage for the day silently or out loud. Read slowly; do not hurry. If you have time, read it again. Then spend some time in silent reflection about any questions or insights the reading prompted. What catches your attention? What word or phrase stops you? What images stay with you? What might God wish for you to receive from this reading?

First Thursday (following Ash Wednesday*)—Romans 5:12-19
Second Thursday—Romans 4:13-25
Third Thursday—1 Corinthians 1:18-25
Fourth Thursday—Ephesians 2:1-10
Fifth Thursday—Hebrews 5:5-10
Sixth Thursday—Isaiah 50:4-9a

*Because Lent begins on Ash Wednesday, the days of the season are counted forward from Ash Wednesday, rather than from the first Sunday in Lent.

SILENT REFLECTION

PRAYERS OF INTERCESSION

O Christ, who is Living Water,
who is deep calling to deep.
You call us to carry
hope to the hopeless,
love to the lost,
and water to the thirsty.
Fill me with your love
to overflowing
that I may have a part in you
and freely give it away.
Amen.

PRAY

- ❧ For orphans
- ❧ For thirsty livestock and endangered species
- ❧ For clean water and plentiful rain
- ❧ For clarity in the decisions you face this day

CLOSING PRAYER OF THANKSGIVING

Spirit of the Living God, I live this day
in the presence of your truth,
by the power of your grace,
with thanksgiving
for the longing I have for you
and the longing you have for me.
Drench me, shape me, move me.
Amen.

BLESSING

Hope in God; for I shall again
      praise him,
  my help and my God.

                —Psalm 42:11b

FRIDAYS OF LENT

WAITING

Return to these pages each Friday (except Good Friday) and begin to pray.

INVOCATION

Wait for the LORD;
> be strong, and let your heart
>> take courage;
> wait for the LORD!

—Psalm 27:14

PRAYER OF CONFESSION

2/16

Like an early bloom before last frost,
like impatient rain from still-blue sky,
so too, O God,
it is hard to wait for you.
I am too hurried to let dawn break,
to let shadows fall,
to let courage root
in the soil of my soul.
But I need to learn to let dawn be dawn
and dusk be dusk,
to let you alone be God,
the God of my life.
Amen.

SCRIPTURE READING

Read the passage for the day silently or out loud. Read slowly; do not hurry. If you have time, read it again. Then spend some time in silent reflection about any questions or insights the reading prompted. What catches your attention? What word or phrase stops you? What images stay with you? What might God wish for you to receive from this reading?

First Friday (following Ash Wednesday*)—1 Peter 3:18-22

Second Friday—Genesis 15:1-12, 17-18

Third Friday—Isaiah 55:1-9

Fourth Friday—Joshua 5:9-12

Fifth Friday—Isaiah 43:16-21

Sixth Friday—Philippians 2:5-11

*Because Lent begins on Ash Wednesday, the days of the season are counted forward from Ash Wednesday, rather than from the first Sunday in Lent.

SILENT REFLECTION

PRAYERS OF INTERCESSION

O loving Christ who waits for us all

to move forward,

to change inward,

to love outward.

Wait now with me as I long and learn to become

more like you.

Guide me to wait with the lost,

to stand with the weak,

to have a heart for the brokenhearted.

Amen.

PRAY

- For all who await news from runaways
- For expectant parents
- For wisdom
- For gentleness toward yourself and others this day

CLOSING PRAYER OF THANKSGIVING

Ah, Holy Spirit, I plant my feet

into the soil of the living God.

I turn my ear toward the voice of the calling Christ.

I lean my life into the wind of holy change.

Be fierce, be gentle,

toss me, turn me,

shape me, dishevel me.

Ah, Holy Spirit,

in gratitude I wait.

Amen.

BLESSING

The LORD is the stronghold of my life;

    of whom shall I be afraid?

        —Psalm 27:1b

SATURDAYS OF LENT

LEARNING

Return to these pages each Saturday (except Holy Saturday) and begin to pray.

INVOCATION

Make me to know your ways, O LORD;
       teach me your paths.
Lead me in your truth, and teach me,
       for you are the God of my salvation;
       for you I wait all day long.
                    —Psalm 25:4-5

PRAYER OF CONFESSION

Eternal God,
my beginning and my ending,
my light by day, my lamp by night.
O One who shapes the ways for me to go
and clears the paths for me to take,
teach me that I may live by love—
not at my pace, but yours.
I hurry; I judge the cover; I read the ending first,
but you call me back to the beginning.
Guide my life over the contours of your Word
that I may learn your ways.
Amen.

SCRIPTURE READING

Read the passage for the day silently or out loud. Read slowly; do not hurry. If you have time, read it again. Then spend some time in silent reflection about any questions or insights the reading prompted. What catches your attention? What word or phrase stops you? What images stay with you? What might God wish for you to receive from this reading?

First Saturday (following Ash Wednesday*)—Romans 10:8b-13
Second Saturday—Philippians 3:17–4:1
Third Saturday—1 Corinthians 10:1-13
Fourth Saturday—2 Corinthians 5:16-21
Fifth Saturday—Philippians 3:4b-14
Sixth Saturday—Mark 10:46-52

*Because Lent begins on Ash Wednesday, the days of the season are counted forward from Ash Wednesday, rather than from the first Sunday in Lent.

SILENT REFLECTION

PRAYERS OF INTERCESSION

Show me the way, O Christ,
to care for those who are hurting,
and weeping, and starving.
Teach me the way, O Christ,
to forgive those who are lying,
and wounding, and excluding.
Be light in the dark
and bread for the journey
that I might become
a living prayer for you in the world.
Amen.

PRAY
- For teachers and mentors
- For all who long to learn the way of peace
- For immigrants and refugees trying to learn new ways
- For openness to God's leading this day

CLOSING PRAYER OF THANKSGIVING

As I leave this time of prayer,
may my thoughts be shaped by love;
may my words be wrapped in kindness;
may my actions be tempered
by the fiery power of the Holy Spirit,
my ever-present teacher and guide.
Amen.

BLESSING

All the paths of the LORD are
       steadfast love and
       faithfulness,
for those who keep his
       covenant and his decrees.

—Psalm 25:10

SUNDAYS IN LENT

SEEKING

Return to these pages each Sunday and begin to pray.

INVOCATION

O God, you are my God, I seek you,
       my soul thirsts for you;
my flesh faints for you,
       as in a dry and weary land
             where there is no water.

. . . .

Because your steadfast love is
       better than life,
my lips will praise you.

                    —Psalm 63:1, 3

PRAYER OF CONFESSION

From the beginning, O God,
you formed light that I might see;
sky that I might look;
earth and sea that I might seek and search.
You formed creatures of every kind—
swarming, flying, swimming, creeping—
that I, O God, might find my place with them;
that I, O God, might praise your making them.
Open my eyes,
too often closed;
clear the sleep from my heart,
too often settled;
that I may seek the blessing of your presence,
O God of my beginning, O God of my life.
Amen.

SCRIPTURE READING**

Read the passage for the day** silently or out loud. Read slowly; do not hurry. If you have time, read it again. Then spend some time in silent reflection about any questions or insights the reading prompted. What catches your attention? What word or phrase stops you? What images stay with you? What might God wish for you to receive from this reading?

	Year A	Year B	Year C
First Sunday	Matthew 4:1-11	Mark 1:9-15	Luke 4:1-13
Second Sunday	John 3:1-17	Mark 8:31-38	Luke 13:31-35
Third Sunday	John 4:5-42	John 2:13-22	Luke 13:1-9
Fourth Sunday	John 9:1-41	John 3:14-21	Luke 15:1-3, 11b-32
Fifth Sunday	John 11:1-45	John 12:20-33	John 12:1-8
Palm Sunday	Matthew 21:1-11	Mark 11:1-11	Luke 19:28-40

**For Lent 2010, use readings from Year C; in 2011, Year A; in 2012, Year B; in 2013, return to Year C; and so on. For more information about assigned lectionary readings for Sundays, see page 25.

SILENT REFLECTION

PRAYERS Of INTERCESSION

May all who feel invisible be seen by you, O Christ.

May all who are discarded believe you treasure them.

May the frightened feel safe;

the bruised, soothed; the forgotten, remembered

in you and by you,

O Christ of the cross;

in me and by me,

O Christ of my prayers.

Amen.

PRAY

- For youth and young people everywhere
- For environmental scientists and ecologists
- For spiritual seekers
- For someone who seeks your approval and love this day

CLOSING PRAYER OF THANKSGIVING

As a child seeks a rising moon,
as a pilgrim seeks a home,
so I seek you, O Bright Spirit.
You are safe harbor by day, safe haven at night.
You are winter's deep quiet
and springtime's light breeze.
What I seek, you provide;
what I need, you offer.
Thanks be to you, O Spirit of life.
Amen.

BLESSING

So I will bless you as long as I live;
    I will lift up my hands and call on your name.
                    —Psalm 63:4

MONDAYS OF LENT

ASKING

Return to these pages each Monday and begin to pray.

INVOCATION

Be merciful to me, O God, be merciful to me,
for in you my soul takes refuge;
in the shadow of your wings I will take refuge,
until the destroying storms pass by.

—Psalm 57:1

PRAYER OF CONFESSION

There is no need unknown to you, O God of my heart.

There is no sigh too soft, no bruise too hidden,

no pretense too clever to keep from you,

for you alone are God—

my breath before I breathe,

my life before I live,

my need before I know

that I need.

Renew my need for you, O God,

and grant me courage to ask.

Amen.

SCRIPTURE READING

Read the passage for the day silently or out loud. Read slowly; do not hurry. If you have time, read it again. Then spend some time in silent reflection about any questions or insights the reading prompted. What catches your attention? What word or phrase stops you? What images stay with you? What might God wish for you to receive from this reading?

First Monday (following Ash Wednesday*)—Genesis 12:1-4a
Second Monday—Exodus 17:1-7
Third Monday—1 Samuel 16:1-13
Fourth Monday—Ezekiel 37:1-14
Fifth Monday—Psalm 118:1-2, 19-29
Sixth Monday (Holy Week)—John 12:1-11

*Because Lent begins on Ash Wednesday, the days of the season are counted forward from Ash Wednesday, rather than from the first Sunday in Lent.

SILENT REFLECTION

PRAYERS OF INTERCESSION

May those who are lost, O Christ,
find a guide in you.
May those who are hungry
find food at your table.
May those who are bullied find courage,
those who are worried find peace,
those who are weary find rest
with you, O Christ,
this day and the next.
Amen.

PRAY

❧ For truth and reconciliation among people who are estranged

❧ For all who must beg for food today

❧ For people who are far from home in a strange land

❧ For what you need this day

CLOSING PRAYER OF THANKSGIVING

O Holy Spirit, promise of God;
O Holy Spirit, breath of heaven;
O Holy Spirit, comforter of all
and friend to any,
stay with me and I with you,
from dawn to dusk to dawn again.
Amen.

BLESSING

For your steadfast love is as high as the heavens;
      your faithfulness extends to the clouds.
               —Psalm 57:10

TUESDAYS
OF LENT

SEARCHING

Return to these pages each Tuesday and begin to pray.

INVOCATION

Search me, O God, and know my heart;
    test me and know my thoughts.
See if there is any wicked way in me,
    and lead me in the way everlasting.
                  —Psalm 139:23-24

PRAYER OF CONFESSION

Somewhere in this day, O God,

let me be surprised by love.

Move me beyond taking life for granted.

Remind me to notice the color of someone's eyes.

Quiet me enough to search,

really search,

the sky—

a palette of golds, blues, and whites—

monochromatic at first glance, but then . . .

Urge me to take off my shoes and to walk upon your earth—

skin to skin, dust to dust.

Amen.

SCRIPTURE READING

Read the passage for the day silently or out loud. Read slowly; do not hurry. If you have time, read it again. Then spend some time in silent reflection about any questions or insights the reading prompted. What catches your attention? What word or phrase stops you? What images stay with you? What might God wish for you to receive from this reading?

First Tuesday (following Ash Wednesday*)—Romans 4:1-5

Second Tuesday—Romans 5:1-11

Third Tuesday—Ephesians 5:8-14

Fourth Tuesday—Romans 8:6-11

Fifth Tuesday—Isaiah 42:1-9

Sixth Tuesday (Holy Week)—John 12:20-36

*Because Lent begins on Ash Wednesday, the days of the season are counted forward from Ash Wednesday, rather than from the first Sunday in Lent.

SILENT REFLECTION

PRAYERS OF INTERCESSION

O Christ who sees the little and the lost:
the child,
the lamb,
the last coin.
Widen my eyes with your compassion;
clear my vision with your justice;
soften my gaze with your tears
for all who need my prayers today.
Amen.

PRAY
- For those in prison who watch for a visitor
- For artists, writers, and dancers who bring beauty to life
- For leaders of nations, cities, and communities
- For someone you know who is searching for an answer this day

CLOSING PRAYER OF THANKSGIVING

There is no curve of this day, O Spirit,

there is no contour of this night,

where you are not with me.

Press me, pull me,

infuse me, immerse me,

for I am gratefully yours.

Amen.

BLESSING

If I take the wings of the morning
　　　　and settle at the farthest limits of the sea,
even there your hand shall lead me,
　　　　and your right hand shall hold me fast.

　　　　　　　　　　—Psalm 139:9-10

WEDNESDAYS OF LENT

PRAYING

Return to these pages each Wednesday (except Ash Wednesday) and begin to pray.

INVOCATION

Give ear, O LORD, to my prayer;
      listen to my cry of supplication.
In the day of my trouble I call on you,
      for you will answer me.

—Psalm 86:6-7

PRAYER OF CONFESSION

On the palm of your hand you write my name, O God.

Through the pages of creation, my life unfolds.

In the chambers of your heart, I have a home, O God,

where every cry is heard, every tear seen,

every thanks

whispered in the dark or sung to the morning

is known to you.

And still, I am slow to thank, to ask, to trust.

O God, who is great and good,

help me to pray.

Amen.

SCRIPTURE READING

Read the passage for the day silently or out loud. Read slowly; do not hurry. If you have time, read it again. Then spend some time in silent reflection about any questions or insights the reading prompted. What catches your attention? What word or phrase stops you? What images stay with you? What might God wish for you to receive from this reading?

First Wednesday (following Ash Wednesday*)—Genesis 17:1-7, 15-16

Second Wednesday—Exodus 20:1-17

Third Wednesday—Numbers 21:4-9

Fourth Wednesday—Jeremiah 31:31-34

Fifth Wednesday—Isaiah 49:1-7

Sixth Wednesday (Holy Week)—John 13:21-32

*Because Lent begins on Ash Wednesday, the days of the season are counted forward from Ash Wednesday, rather than from the first Sunday in Lent.

SILENT REFLECTION

PRAYERS OF INTERCESSION

Teach me to pray, O Christ,

that your kingdom will come,

that your will be done,

that earth will become like heaven

for the hurt and the hurting,

the wounded and warring,

the hated and hating.

Teach me to pray, O Christ, for the power is yours.

Amen.

PRAY

- ♪ For people who pray every day
- ♪ For custodians and groundskeepers who tend to places of prayer
- ♪ For all who sit with the dying, the sick, and the grieving
- ♪ For a forgiving heart this day

CLOSING PRAYER OF THANKSGIVING

Bless, O Spirit,
the ways I choose this day.
Bless, O Spirit,
the words I say.
Bless, O Spirit,
the forgiveness I give,
the bread I share,
the prayers I pray,
that I may become your blessing for another.
Amen.

BLESSING

Teach me your way, O LORD,
    that I may walk in your truth;
    give me an undivided heart to revere your name.
          —Psalm 86:11

MAUNDY THURSDAY

TRUSTING

INVOCATION

I love the LORD, because he has heard
> my voice and my supplications.
Because he inclined his ear to me,
> therefore I will call on him as long as I live.
>> —Psalm 116:1-2

PRAYER OF CONFESSION

O God, who loved the world

so much

that you gave away your Son

so that all might see, so that each might know,

so that I might trust in your never-failing love.

And yet, O God, we loved

so little,

that we gave him back to you.

Lord, have mercy.

Christ, have mercy.

Lord, have mercy.

Amen.

SCRIPTURE READING

Read the passage for the day silently or out loud. Read slowly; do not hurry. If you have time, read it again. Then spend some time in silent reflection about any questions or insights the reading prompted. What catches your attention? What word or phrase stops you? What images stay with you? What might God wish for you to receive from this reading?

Maundy Thursday—John 13:1-17, 31b-35

SILENT REFLECTION

PRAYERS OF INTERCESSION

Into your hands, O Christ,
my life and my loves.
Into your hands, O Lord,
my enemies and friends.
Into your hands, O Lamb,
the bread and the cup
for the broken and blessed,
for the wanting and willing.
From your hands to my hands,
entrust now in prayer.
Amen.

PRAY

- For children around the world
- For animals large and small, especially those in danger
- For those who work in law, medicine, or finance
- For deepened trust in God's love for you this day

CLOSING PRAYER OF THANKSGIVING

Under the edge of darkness, O Holy Spirit,
you are a trace of light.
You are a peace that startles my fear.
You are a promise that shatters my doubt.
Stay with me, O Spirit,
in my coming and going,
in my doing and believing,
in my trying and trusting,
for now and forever.
Amen.

BLESSING

Gracious is the LORD, and righteous;
     our God is merciful.

—Psalm 116:5

GOOD FRIDAY

HOPING

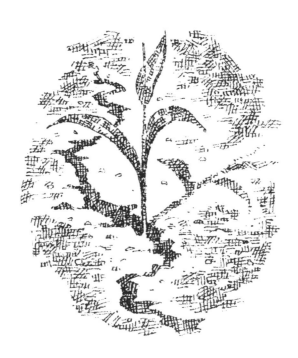

INVOCATION

I wait for the LORD, my soul waits,
     and in his word I hope;
my soul waits for the LORD
       more than those who watch for the morning,
       more than those who watch for the morning.

—Psalm 130:5-6

PRAYER OF CONFESSION

God of this day, forgive my pretense:
that I know, when I do not;
that I care, when I am callous;
that I see, when far too often,
I cover my eyes, turn my head, walk away.
God of this moment, transform my shortcomings:
that I can be trusted, when I sometimes betray;
that I can believe, when I often deny;
that I can hope, when deep within,
I bargain with hopelessness.
Renew me, O God, by your far-reaching grace.
Restore, me, O God, to your life-giving truth
that the kingdom, power, and glory are yours
at this moment, on this day, for all time.
Amen.

SCRIPTURE READING

Read the passage for the day silently or out loud. Read slowly; do not hurry. If you have time, read it again. Then spend some time in silent reflection about any questions or insights the reading prompted. What catches your attention? What word or phrase stops you? What images stay with you? What might God wish for you to receive from this reading?

Good Friday—John 18:1–19:42

SILENT REFLECTION

PRAYERS OF INTERCESSION

May those without hope take heart in you, O Christ.

May those with no home find shade at your right hand.

May those near the end see beginnings;

may those at the last become first.

At the foot of your cross, O Christ,

I come in prayer.

O Christ, be my help,

O Christ, be our hope.

Amen.

PRAY

❧ For those who struggle with memory loss and for their caregivers

❧ For ministers, priests, and church leaders who offer words of hope

❧ For victims of betrayal, oppression, or violence and for the perpetrators

❧ For faith, hope, and love to shape your words this day

CLOSING PRAYER OF THANKSGIVING

A whisper you are in the silence,

a flame in the dark.

You are birdsong at daybreak,

first star at night.

Come, Holy Spirit,

my hope and my guide.

Come, Holy Spirit,

my advocate, my friend.

Amen.

BLESSING

For with the LORD there is steadfast love,

and with him is great power to redeem.

—Psalm 130:7b

HOLY SATURDAY

BELIEVING

INVOCATION

Why are you cast down, O my soul,
     and why are you disquieted within me?
Hope in God; for I shall again praise him,
     my help and my God.

—Psalm 42:11

PRAYER OF CONFESSION

I want to believe, O God,
that the morning will push back the night.
I want to believe, O God,
that the stone will roll fully away.
I want to believe, O God,
that the tomb will hold only angels,
that the women will come to behold,
that the others will come to believe;
and I, along with them, O God . . .
God, help my unbelief.
Amen.

SCRIPTURE READING

Read the passage for the day silently or out loud. Read slowly; do not hurry. If you have time, read it again. Then spend some time in silent reflection about any questions or insights the reading prompted. What catches your attention? What word or phrase stops you? What images stay with you? What might God wish for you to receive from this reading?

Holy Saturday—Matthew 27:62-66

SILENT REFLECTION

PRAYERS OF INTERCESSION

O Christ of the cross,
of the grave, of the road.
Before me, behind me,
beside me, beloved by me.
Where you have gone, let me go:
to the poor and the sick.
As you have cared, let me care:
for the doubting and the broken.
When you have prayed, let me pray:
at daybreak and nightfall.
Today, tomorrow, forever, O Christ,
this time, next time, all time. Amen.

PRAY

❧ For missionaries who share Christ's compassion

❧ For all who grieve the death of a child

❧ For those who work the night shift

❧ For joyful obedience to follow Christ this day

CLOSING PRAYER OF THANKSGIVING

Once-still leaves now flutter,
thanks to you, O breath of life.
Once-set stone now shifts,
by the power of your love.
Once-hard hearts now soften,
thanks to you, O flame of Spirit.
Come quickly, come now.
Alleluia,
Amen.

BLESSING

Hope in God; for I shall again praise him,
     my help and my God.

              —Psalm 42:11b

session plans for a six-week prayer group

These six group sessions are designed to last for about one hour each. The pattern of reading, prayer, and conversation remains the same in each session so that group members will, after the first week, know what to expect. Also, to help members feel part of the group process, each session includes elements that members may be asked to prepare and lead.

BEFORE THE GROUP GATHERS

There are six Sundays during the season of Lent, the last of which is Palm/Passion Sunday. As long as your last prayer group session takes place on or before Palm/Passion Sunday, it does not matter what day of the week you choose to schedule your group meeting. If you choose to meet on a day other than Sunday, schedule your first session during the week of Ash Wednesday, before the first Sunday in Lent.

The content of the prayer group sessions is based upon but not the same as the daily prayers found in *The Awkward Season*. Be sure that group members have a copy of the book at least a week before the first session. Encourage them to begin using the daily prayers during their personal prayer time. Explain that no other preparation is needed for the group sessions except arriving in an attitude of prayer.

Preparing for the Sessions

Leader preparation for each session is minimal: gathering the materials for each session (see page 98) and contacting two group members in advance to read the designated psalm (responsive reading from the Psalter) and Gospel text for the upcoming session. If you wish, you can rotate the leadership each week among group members. If you choose this route, give group members ample notice about which session they will lead.

Each week "Jesus, Remember Me"* will be sung at the end of the session. If you prefer not to lead music, ask someone who is musically inclined to lead the group in singing. Group members will quickly learn the simple tune. If hymnals are not available for group sessions, provide photocopies of the words of the song and the psalm (photocopies must include all copyright information about the source). Also, each group member needs a Bible or a photocopy of the Gospel reading.

*"Jesus, Remember Me," based on Luke 23:42, is a song from the Taizé community; you can find it in *The United Methodist Hymnal* (no. 488), *Upper Room Worshipbook* (no. 382), or at www.giamusic.com.

SETTING UP FOR THE SESSIONS

Leader: Arrive at least fifteen minutes before each session to be sure the room is open and to arrange chairs in a circle. In the center of the circle of chairs, place a small table or bench draped with a purple cloth. The table should be large enough to hold a large pillar candle placed in the center and surrounded by several small, inexpensive votive candles (each group member will light two votives during the prayer time). These candles will be reused over the course of the group meetings; have a few extra candles available. Bring a lighter.

Each week at the beginning of the session, light the center candle to remind everyone that Christ is also present. Because votives will be used during the session, you will need to have some means of lighting them as well, either from the center candle or with a lighter.

Elements of Each Session

Gathering and Welcome *(3–5 minutes)*

Lighting the Christ Candle *(1 minute)*

Opening Words of Praise and Prayer *(1 minute)*

Responsive Reading of the Psalm *(1–2 minutes)*

Silent Reflection *(2 minutes)*

Prayers of Confession *(5 minutes)*

Gospel Reading *(1–3 minutes)*

Silent Reflection *(2 minutes)*

Conversation Prompted by the Gospel Reading *(10 minutes)*

Prayers of Intercession *(10 minutes)*

The Lord's Prayer *(1 minute)*

Closing Song *(1 minute)*

Benediction and Sending Forth *(1 minute)*

The Peace *(2–3 minutes)*

Materials Needed for Each Session

Each group member needs to bring a copy of *The Awkward Season*. Leader, gather the following materials:

- hymnals with the selected Psalter reading for the week and the words of the closing song, "Jesus, Remember Me" (no. 488, *The United Methodist Hymnal*), or photocopies of the *text only* of the reading and song
- Bibles or photocopies of the selected Gospel reading for the week
- small table or bench
- purple cloth to drape over the table or bench
- large pillar candle to use as the Christ candle
- enough inexpensive votive candles for every group member to light two each week
- lighter for the candles
- photocopies of "An Order for Lenten Praise and Prayer" (pages 99–105) for group members who forget to bring their copy of this book
- watch or clock to monitor the prayer and conversation times during the session

An order for Lenten praise and prayer

This order can be used each week. Only the responsive reading from the Psalms and the Gospel reading will change, and these are listed at the end of the order (see page 105).

GATHERING AND WELCOME
Group members greet one another as they find a seat and enter into this time of prayer.

LIGHTING THE CHRIST CANDLE
The leader lights the center candle in silence as a sign of Christ's presence with the group.

OPENING WORDS OF PRAISE AND PRAYER

Leader: The grace of the Lord Jesus Christ be with you.

People: **And also with you.**

All: **Thanks be to God. Amen.**

RESPONSIVE READING OF THE PSALM
Read the assigned psalm slowly and responsively.

SILENT REFLECTION

In silence, reflect on the psalm that was read. Do not rush through this time. Use at least two full minutes to meditate and pray.

PRAYERS OF CONFESSION

The leader invites group members to enter into a period of silent confession. Each group member, at some time during this five-minute period, is encouraged to light one votive candle as a sign of trust in God's forgiving mercy and grace. To begin, the following or similar words are spoken:

Leader: Friends, let us place before God anything that we have allowed to come between us and our relationship with God . . . between us and our relationship with our neighbors . . . between us and our relationship with creation. Let us confess to God what we have done and what we have not done . . . what we have said and what we have not said. Let us pray: Lord, have mercy.

People: **Christ, have mercy.**

Leader: Lord, have mercy. Let us enter into silence.

Group members spend time in silent prayer, each lighting one candle at any time. When the five-minute period is almost complete, the following words are repeated to close the prayers:

Leader:	Lord, have mercy.
People:	**Christ, have mercy.**
All:	**Lord, have mercy.**

GOSPEL READING

A member of the group slowly reads the assigned Gospel passage. If desired, a second reading of the text may be offered.

SILENT REFLECTION

In silence, reflect on the scripture that was read. Do not rush through this time. Use at least two full minutes to meditate and pray.

CONVERSATION PROMPTED BY THE GOSPEL READING

The leader invites the group to reflect together for about ten minutes on the Gospel story they heard. Encourage group members to listen well to one another and to make room for anyone who wishes to speak. Permission to remain silent is always given. This conversation can begin with the following or similar questions from the leader:

What does this story say about Jesus?

What does this story say about humankind?

PRAYERS OF INTERCESSION

The leader introduces ten minutes of time to be spent in intercessory prayer using the following or similar words and categories. Invite group members to name people, concerns, and needs aloud or silently after each category is named. There is no need to hurry through these prayers: take your time to recall news stories, local needs, distant friends, and dear loved ones.

Leader: We have come to a time to offer prayers on behalf of others, on behalf of the world, and on behalf of all creation. Together, let us pray for:

Family members . . .

Friends . . .

People in the news . . .

Places in trouble . . .

Circumstances that break God's heart . . .

People we miss; the communion of saints . . .

Healing of creation . . .

Christ's church . . .

When the ten minutes have almost passed, the leader lights one votive candle as a sign of being a bearer of Christ's light into the world. Each group member does the same until all candles have been lit.

THE LORD'S PRAYER
(Spoken in unison.)

Our Father in heaven,

hallowed be your name.

your kingdom come,

your will be done, on earth as in heaven.

Give us today our daily bread.

Forgive us our sins

as we forgive those who sin against us.

Save us from the time of trial

and deliver us from evil.

For the kingdom, the power, and the glory are yours

now and forever. Amen.

CLOSING SONG

"Jesus, Remember Me" (no. 488, The United Methodist Hymnal*) or another short song or chorus may be quietly sung several times with or without accompaniment.*

BENEDICTION AND SENDING FORTH

Leader: The grace of the Lord Jesus Christ,
            and the love of God,
            and the communion of the Holy Spirit
            be with you all.

People: **Amen.**

THE PEACE

Group members exchange signs and words of Christ's peace as all depart.

weekly psalter and gospel readings

	Psalm / No. in UMH*	**Gospel Reading**
Week 1	Psalm 91 / No. 810	Luke 4:1-13
Week 2	Psalm 27 / No. 758	Mark 8:31-38
Week 3	Psalm 19 / No. 750	John 2:13-22
Week 4	Psalm 32 / No. 766	Luke 15:1-3, 11b-32
Week 5	Psalm 51:1-17 / No. 785	John 12:1-8
Week 6	Psalm 118:14-29 / No. 839	Matthew 21:1-11

* From *The United Methodist Hymnal* (Nashville, TN: United Methodist Publishing House, 1989).

Bibliography

Job, Rueben P., and Norman Shawchuck. *A Guide to Prayer for All Who Seek God.* Nashville, TN: Upper Room Books, 2003.

Job, Rueben P., and Norman Shawchuck. *A Guide to Prayer for Ministers and Other Servants.* Nashville, TN: The Upper Room, 1983.

Newell, J. Philip. *Celtic Prayers from Iona.* Mahwah, NJ: Paulist Press, 1997.

Rowlett, Martha Graybeal. *Praying Together: Forming Prayer Ministries in Your Congregation.* Nashville, TN: Upper Room Books, 2002.

Schaper, Donna, and Carole Ann Camp. *Labyrinths from the Outside In: Walking to Spiritual Insight—A Beginner's Guide.* Woodstock, VT: SkyLight Paths Publishing, 2000.

The United Methodist Hymnal. Nashville, TN: The United Methodist Publishing House, 1989.

about the author

Pamela C. Hawkins serves as managing editor of *Weavings: A Journal of the Christian Spiritual Life.* An ordained elder in the United Methodist Church, she previously served in local church and seminary settings in Tennessee and North Carolina. As often as her schedule permits, Pam leads small groups and retreats about matters of the Christian spiritual life. She is the author of *Simply Wait: Cultivating Stillness in the Season of Advent* (Upper Room Books, 2007) and coeditor of *Courageous Spirit: Voices from Women in Ministry* (Upper Room Books, 2005).

Pam and her husband, Ray, live in Nashville, Tennessee. They are the parents of two adult sons, Erick and Phil; and grandparents to Tyler, Hayden, Harper, and Emerson.

using a finger labyrinth with lenten prayers

BEFORE YOU BEGIN

- Open *The Awkward Season* to the prayers for today and your Bible to the assigned reading. Place bookmarks in both so that you can easily turn to the readings.
- Open the flap at the back of this book to reveal the finger labyrinth. Place your finger at the opening of the labyrinth path (1). Read the Invocation for the day and be open to encountering God during this time of prayer.

FIRST MOVEMENT: RELEASING (CONFESSION)

Read the Prayer of Confession silently or aloud. When finished, slowly move your finger forward along the labyrinth. Move at your own pace toward the center (2). Let the words of the prayers of Invocation and Confession stay with you.

Quiet your mind as you move through the labyrinth. Make room for emotions and stirrings that arise. What needs to be changed, forgiven, cleared, confronted, or healed in your life? Offer these situations to God as you move forward.

Second Movement: Receiving (Centering)

When you reach the center (2), rest your finger there for a moment before you turn to and read the Scripture Reading for the day.

When you are ready, read the passage slowly, as if you have never read it before. Center on God's Word and be open to what God reveals to you through the reading. Return your finger to the center of the labyrinth and reflect on the passage and what it holds for you.

Third Movement: Returning (Intercession)

As you prepare to leave the labyrinth, place your finger at the same opening in the center where you entered (3). Now, read the Prayers of Intercession for the day and when finished, begin to move your finger back along the same path on which you entered. Let the intercessory prayers stay with you, and add to them as you make the turns and move along the pattern back out of the labyrinth. Be mindful of people and circumstances in the world in need of your prayers. Hold each in your heart for a part of the journey outward.

When You Have Finished

As you lift your finger from the labyrinth's end, offer thanks to God with the Blessing for the day or another prayer of your choosing.